For Victor

With thanks to Vincent Pomarède, Gérard de Wallens,
Céline Julhiet-Charvet and Anne de Margerie.

Published by Peter Bedrick Books
2112 Broadway, New York, NY 10023

Layout and design: Thomas Gravemaker, X-Act

ISBN 0-87226-477-7
CIP Data is available from the Library of Congress
Peter Bedrick Books and the swan logo are trademarks
of Peter Bedrick Books Inc.

Printed in Mexico
5 4 3 2 1 96 97 98 99 00
First American Edition

Corot
from A to Z

Caroline Larroche

Translated from the French by
Claudia Zoe Bedrick

PETER BEDRICK BOOKS

NEW YORK

Contents

Colisée
Colosseum

Doutes
Doubts

En forêt
In the Forest

Folie
Madness

Grand enfant
Big Child

Minuscules
Miniatures

Nymphes
Nymphs

Ode à Marietta
Ode to Marietta

Petit Papa Corot
Little Father Corot

Que d'hésitations!
Such Hesitations!

Wallet

fauX
False

Yport

aZur
Azure

Crédits photos
Acknowledgments

À deux pas du pont

Near the Bridge

On July 16, 1796, in Paris, near the beautiful Pont-Royal bridge, Jean-Baptiste Corot is born. He will be called by his middle name, Camille.

His parents own a fashionable boutique where they sell ribbons, pens and hats.

The family lives quite comfortably. The first images seen by the baby Camille are of the Seine and its bridges.

He does not yet know that one day his paint brush will transform those works of stone into painted masterpieces.

His parents do not give any thought to making him an artist. As far as they are concerned, he will become a lawyer or a doctor.

As an adolescent, however, Camille pursues his studies absent-mindedly, while he draws constantly in secret.

He wants to become a painter. After some hesitation, he reveals this to his parents.

"Impossible!" declares his inflexible father, who arranges for some clothing merchants to take Camille on, as a delivery boy.

As it turns out, this job provides a wonderful opportunity for Camille to wander through the streets, pencil in hand.

Marie Corot, Camille's mother, painted by her son in 1845.

Bon voyage !

It becomes obvious that Camille Corot will never be a good clothier, when he dares to touch materials with hands covered with paint. His father, resigned to this fact, accepts that his son will become a painter. At last, Camille can seize his pencils and paint-brushes freely. He is 26 years old.

In his parents house in the Ville d'Avray, he arranges a bedroom-studio.

A study of a Roman warrior done at the Louvre.

Camille goes less frequently to the Louvre than most young painters.
He prefers to walk up and down the wharves and to explore the forests, the Normandy countryside and its seashores.
He knows, however, that it is in Italy that a good painter must evelop his skill. To his surprise, his father offers to send him there, but on one condition: Camille must leave behind a portrait of himself. The young painter fulfills his task.
Soon his self portrait will take its place on the wall, and Camille, deliriously happy, will take his seat in the stage-coach for Rome.

Detail of the self portrait which Camille leaves his parents.

Colisée

Colosseum

Camille is not unmoved by the charms of the young Italian girls.

In Rome, Camille moves into a neighborhood of foreigners, near the Spanish steps. There he finds other painters who, like himself, have come to work in the countryside according to tradition. At the cafe Greco, the scene is lively. People joke and sing and Camille is the life and soul of the party. Nevertheless, he works steadily. Soon, without really knowing it, he paints his first masterpieces. He captures the ruins of the Colosseum, the gardens and the bridges, and always the play of air and light. In the dazzling countryside surrounding Rome, he observes and seeks to understand the movement of the sky. His friends already call him "our Master."

Camille as sketched by one of his friends.

Doutes

Doubts

Camille had thought to stay in Rome for only a year, but already he has spent two springs marveling at its beauties. He paints all that is offered to him: golden ruins, lively city scenes, and expanses of wild nature.

On wood, paper, and pasteboard, he juxtaposes opaque masses and little patches of light. As shadows lengthen, his paintings gain in depth.

All of Italy is there, absolute and eternal. Nevertheless, his enthusiasm is mixed with doubts. He recognizes that his comrades do not paint exactly as he does.

Shadows and light on the Roman countryside.

"At moments, my way of painting seems to me quite awful," he writes to Abel, his childhood friend. "Never paint if you wish to live peacefully."

When he finally leaves Rome, in the Autumn of 1828, Camille does not suspect that his trunks contain numerous little treasures.

Camille is 29 when he paints this landscape.

En forêt

In the Forest

With its large stone boulders and its oak trees, which are hundreds of years old, the forests of Fontainebleau, near Paris, remind Camille of the grandeur of the Italian landscape.

In the heart of the forest, at the Inn Ganne, he meets again his comrades from Rome, the painters Bertin and d'Aligny. Many other painters are also there, for Fontainebleau is a fashionable spot, a veritable open-air studio.

In the forest, Camille does a number of ink sketches.

Fascinated, Camille slowly paints green and brown rocks,
the oranges of the sky, the ochre and greens of the tall
trees. He feels nature's majesty resonating within him.
Camille sees precisely.
His paintbrush moves with feeling.
Modest as he is, he says, "I paint for the little birds."

A quarry of stones in Fontainebleau.

Folie

Madness

Camille hangs his small paintings of Italy in his studio. He calls them his "exercises," even though he is already a great painter. It is at this time that his father suggests that he marry.

Alexina, with whom Corot was in love.

Several of the small paintings which Corot brings back from Italy.

Gently, Camille makes it clear to him that he does not wish to do so. "I was not alone just now. In the next room, a lovely girl is hidden who enters and exits at my wish. It is madness, my invisible companion." He has decided. He has chosen his "madness": painting, his companion for life. From then on, he works ceaselessly, in Paris during the winter and in the country when the weather is good.

He is equally content to paint field-mice and city rats.

He also paints beautiful portraits. Camille is happy.

For better or for worse, he has become a painter.

Grand enfant

Big Child

Camille's parents do not take him seriously. He is too happy, too carefree to be a real painter.

His mother asks herself what talent this forty year-old, who always goes around in a smock and muddy shoes, might have. His father is full of contempt.

Camille does not even earn enough to pay for his paints.

It is enough for Mr. Corot to read a bad review of his son's work in the newspaper for him to persuade his wife, "You see, he isn't good for anything!"

In response to one of Camille's paintings inspired by the beautiful verses of the young poet, Théophile Gautier, his father cuttingly remarks, "This poet is only some unknown." And when he learns that a certain Corot has been decorated with the Legion of Honor, he rejoices for himself.

The "big kid" also knows how to be serious.

He cannot imagine that this Corot might be his son.
The gentle Camille, however, does not waver.
He loves his parents, and above all, he loves to paint.

We know only this portrait of Camille's father. When he dies in 1847, Camille is 53 years old.

Histoires

Homer and the Shepherds, painted for the Salon of 1845.

Stories from History

At this time, the public's preference is for large paintings which depict Biblical and mythological scenes, little stories from history.

They are seen by the hundreds at the Salon, the great Parisian exhibition where every painter must show his work.

Alone in his studio, Camille prepares for the event each year.

d'Histoire

Using elements from his open-air studies, he takes from here and there the form of a rock, a tree and a piece of Roman ruin.

In accordance with the established rules, Camille conscientiously "assembles" a painting from all those different pieces.

He does it less well than he thinks. His material becomes superficial and his colors too bright. Camille fools himself by putting his talent in the service of history. When he abandons the fields, his genius abandons him.

In Venice.

Italie toujours

Italy forever

Camille is disappointed. Despite his efforts to please, praise is cool. He is recognized as a "good painter," nothing more. Some critics remark that he seems to restrain his talent, a nice way of saying that he doesn't have any.

The truth is that Camille's genius lies elsewhere. It can be found in his "exercises," which he brought back from Italy. In 1834, Camille can no longer keep from returning there. He passes the summer in Tuscany, with his friend Grandjean, and

Lake Como, in the north of Italy.

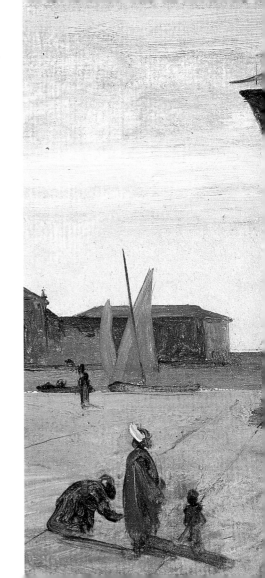

he lingers for a month in Volterra, because the country is so "magnificent." When he discovers Venice, Camille is bewitched by its watery light, which he paints.

And when the mists of silver or pale vermilion envelop the lakes of the North, Camille becomes a poet of landscape. His eye is sharpened. He has become a great painter.

Grandjean, Corot's travelling companion.

Jour après jour

Day after Day

Camille lives a simple life. He doesn't need much to be content: a card game, an evening with his parents, a game of bingo with a few friends.

He also enjoys going to Rosny where his good friend, Abel Osmond, has a chateau surrounded by a beautiful park.

Maurice

Little Louis

At Rosny, Camille is able to paint from morning to night. A small dilapidated house has even been turned into a studio for him.

When Abel dies in 1840, one of his cousins, François Robert, opens his home in Mantes to Camille.

In the company of little Louis and Maurice, the children of the family, his joy, which departed at his friend's death, returns.

Arising at dawn, he again goes out walking, with his sack on his back and his paintbrush in hand.

Day after day, keeping his distance from the laborers, the painter speaks with the trees, the clouds and the sea.

Camille paints Rosny Chateau in 1840.

A boat grounded on the beach of Trouville.

In the Jura mountains

Like a mathematician who takes the measure of his universe, Camille travels each year to the four corners of France or to foreign countries.
He likes to be loved, and his friends, more and more numerous, argue over his company.

In Avignon

Kilomètres

Kilometers

On the Morvan hills.

During the summer of 1841, he covers the Morvan on foot. The following year, he goes to the Jura mountains in Switzerland. In 1843, he is in Rome and in 1854, he discovers Holland. When he is not in Alençon, he is welcomed in Arras or Saint-Lô. There is so much light to be seized! Each summer brings a new journey, always one of friendship. From North to South, his palette reveals its different colors.

It is difficult to follow a traveling painter.

La Rochelle

As the seasons change, Camille celebrates the changing light. In the summer of 1851, he travels to Normandy, and then into Brittany, where he goes to La Rochelle.

He arrives there on July 29, still sad over the death of "the lovely lady," which is what he calls his mother. Soon, however, the painter overcomes his grief.

Here, everything enchants: the majesty of the ancient towers, the liveliness of the docks, the clanking of stays. Settled on the ground floor of a house which faces the port to the Atlantic, Camille achieves a master stroke. His views of La Rochelle, of blond powders, pearly azure, and silvery vapors, are a iracle of delicacy and simplicity. Sure of himself and determined this time not to hide the true talent for which the critics clamor, Corot presents one of his paintings at the Salon of 1852.

At the base of the tower, the water is like a mirror.

Minuscules

Miniatures

A farm in Bourgogne.

They are tiny, the spots of color which show here and there in Corot's landscapes. Is it only a drop of paint which has fallen from his paintbrush? No, Corot is too sure of his hand. All these spots are miniature people—peasants, villagers, shepherds, and their animals.

Light as the imprint of a feather, they enliven the view of a road, warming the slightly heavy half-tints which Corot loves.

A touch of blue here is a young peasant holding a bundle of sticks. A drop of white there, a hen with her chicks scratching about for food. Of three red dashes, two are women in neck scarves busying themselves on the riverbank.

They are miniatures, the little people of Corot.

As with his earlier canvases, Corot often chooses to work in small dimensions, on surfaces barely larger than two hands or an open notebook.

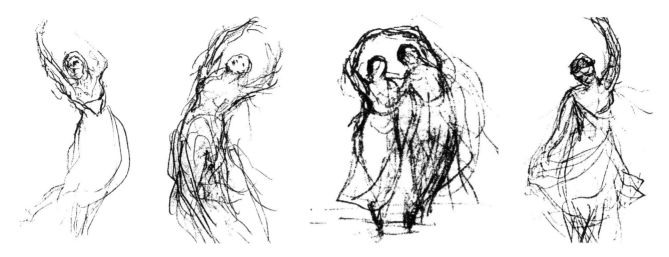

Nymphes

Nymphs

Several times a week, with a notebook in his pocket, Corot goes to the theater.
He saves his Sundays for the opera. The music makes him joyous.
"His face brightens and his eye shines," say his friends. He loves the deep symphonies
of Beethoven, the light sonatas of Mozart and the thrilling operas of Gluck.
In the darkness of the hall, Corot is happy, and without a sound, he scribbles.

A circle of nymphs,
one morning...

His pencil at the ready, Corot captures a dance step, a light leap.
Corot allows himself to be enchanted. Upon return to his studio, he gives birth on canvas to gracious circles of nymphs.
The small gods of the forests and the springs dance beneath his paintbrush.
The colors shimmer in the rustling lightness of the leaves. The atmosphere becomes vaporous and fragile. Corot dreams and his dreams transport him.

Ode à Marietta

Ode to Marietta

Here you see Marietta. Corot is very proud and willingly shows his *Odalisque,* painted in Rome in 1843. Who is Marietta? Simply a model? A friend?
We do not know. Only the front of the painting has preserved her name and her gaze.

Not simply a nude, it is a portrait of Marietta that Corot has painted.
Against white linen, her skin renders the most delicate nuances of mother-of-pearl.
Each tone—large flat tints of rose, ivory, light copper—is just right.
Corot knows that he can be proud of Marietta.

A look, a presence...

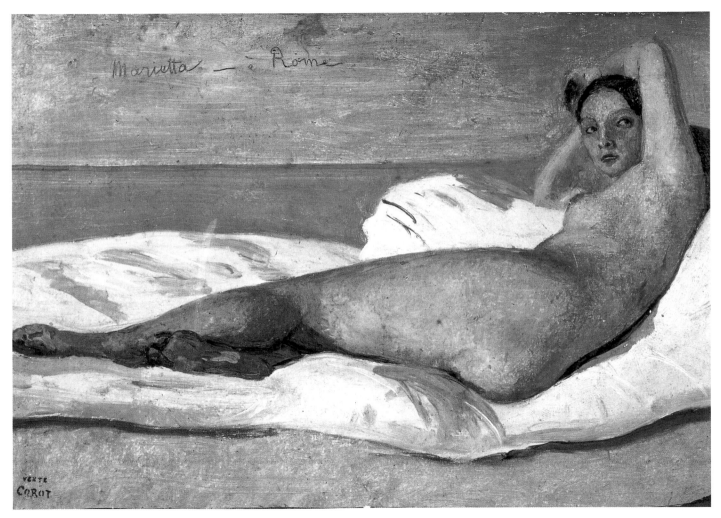

Petit Papa Corot

Little Father Corot

Corot moves through life as he does through his painting, filled with love. For all, he has become "Little Papa Corot."

Wherever he is found, he has a cotton cap on his head and a pipe in his mouth. Goodness nestles in the corners of his smile, and his squinting eyes are attentive and mischievous.

Children, the very little ones, are his friends. He has a pure heart. Ever since his paintings have started to sell, Little Father Corot has helped to relieve the misery around him.

From poor painters, he buys paintings at a price

Corot in his studio, as seen by a painter friend.

Octave, one of
Corot's little friends.

higher than their value. He also pays their doctors' bills and their rent. If one of his models decides to marry, he offers her a dowry. Corot does not spend his money; he gives it away.

His maid, the worried Adèle, finds him reckless. Each time, Corot timidly excuses himself, saying, "My work is more beautiful when I give to others. It is because I give that I am able to paint the little branches of trees."

Corot gave a dowry to this young bride.

Que
Such

The critics begin to recognize Corot's talent. However, the small art world, which makes and breaks success, remains a little blind. At the Universal Exhibition of 1855, Corot exhibits six paintings. Only a few painters, the most important of whom is Delacroix, vote for him to receive a first class medal. Will he be denied the prize? A stormy debate breaks out in the jury. Some continue to hesitate. Finally, Corot's paintings triumph over all doubts. Within the art world, his

The Emperor at the Universal Exhibition.

d'hésitations !

Hesitations!

talent has been recognized.
He is 60 years old.
The moment of
consecration is when
Napoleon III, the French
Emperor, is offered a Corot
for his personal collection.
However, the tastes of the
period are strange: ten
years later, in 1865, the jury will prefer
Cabanel, the most conventional of
painters.
Corot will have to be content with a
second class medal.

The Dell, one of the paintings
exhibited in 1855.

Detail of the painting purchased
by Napoleon III.

Refus

Refusal

Henceforth, Corot is considered one of the great French landscape painters.

The critics finally sing his praises.

"Lead me, dear Master, into the beautiful countryside," writes the celebrated journalist, Zacharie Astruc.

Merchants flock to the door of his studio. He is even invited to enter the Institute, that "sacred place" which admits only the finest of the nation. It is a great honor. Corot, nevertheless, refuses.

"The wise man," he says, "is happy in oblivion." What could he do at the Institute anyway, the painter who loves only the fields?

The little man in the dark shirt is probably Corot.

The Bridge of Mantes, one of Corot's masterpieces.

All of his happiness is there: on the banks of a river, along a winding path, in front of a cluster of trees. On the fringes of the artistic movements of his time, he is simply, "the happiest of men."

Singes

Monkeys

The graceful gesture of a young girl combing her hair.

In a cabinet, hidden from view, is where Corot keeps his little portraits.

The rare people to whom he shows them, burst out laughing: How frightful they are, they might even be called "monkeys"!

Corot, almost frightened by such a reaction, closes the door and holds his tongue.

Inwardly, however, he chuckles. "I compose like a school boy, I draw like a simpleton and I paint like a monkey, that is clear... and yet, I am among the number one painters!"

For some time now, he has been painting numerous portraits. He has common people, children, servants, friends, and strangers pose for him. Corot feels confident with them.
He commands the model to move, even to walk or to jump, if that appeals to him.
The position interests him as much as the gaze.
It is from the base of color that the light of the gaze is realized.

With a pearl on her forehead, the young Berthe becomes a Renaissance beauty. Quite a strange monkey...

Tant de souvenirs

So Many Memories

Corot is no longer able to wander around the countryside as before. He suffers from gout. It is painful for him to walk.

Forced to remain in his studio, he gazes at his cherished studies and remembers. He calls nature to mind, which he feels has thanked him each day "with a sunny smile or a gust of wind."

Detail of the painting, *Souvenir of Mortefontaine.*

He remembers Italy and the regions of France which he visited again and again. And he paints. *Souvenir of Ville-d'Avray, Souvenir of the Lake of Nemi, Souvenir of Castelgandolfo....*

Near a pond, a young girl raises herself up on her toes. The light of morning is transparent. Transparency wears a veil of nostalgia.

It is so wonderful to remember when one is old.

Un ami

A Friend

October 14, 1865. Constant Dutilleux has just died. Corot is in a state of bewilderment.

Dutilleux was a man of taste, one of the first to buy, in 1847, a painting from Corot. He also was one of the first to be seized by a passion for Corot's painting. A painter himself, he opened a studio in Arras where Corot often went to join him. Together they painted and made engravings.

After Dutilleux's death, Corot remains

The two friends, Corot and Dutilleux, as drawn by Alfred Robaut.

Corot engraved this self-portrait at Dutilleux's home.

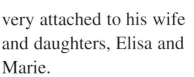

very attached to his wife and daughters, Elisa and Marie.

He continues to visit the North frequently, staying in Douai at the home of Alfred Robaut, Elisa's husband. Their relations are so affectionate that Alfred undertakes to write the life of Camille.

He questions the old painter about his past and observes him at work. Little by little, Alfred becomes the memory of Camille Corot.

Ville-d'Avray

Ville-d'Avray feels far away from the world, far from any noise.
It is a port of call for all voyages.
For more than fifty years, the family house has been Corot's refuge.
Always faithful to that place, he settles in for anywhere from several days, to a few weeks, or even a month or two.
There he is at home.

Corot in Ville-d'Avray, as painted by Daumier.

Ville-d'Avray where Corot and his sister share the family house.

Not so much within the house, which he calls "my sister's home," as on the banks of his old pond, under the shadows of the calm trees. Now more than seventy years old, he has not ceased to marvel at the misty sunrises, the rose sunsets, and his "cherished little branches."

He is called the Master of the Ville-d'Avray. For some time already, the Ville-d'Avray has been seen to resemble a painting by Corot.

Wallet

As so many others, Paul Wallet, a collector and amateur painter, allows himself to be seduced by the simplicity of the Master.

He receives Corot frequently at Voisinlieu, where he lives on a secluded property traversed by a river. One day, Corot decides to paint the path which leads to the small village of Marissel.

It is a spring morning. Nature is still undecided. Accompanied by a young student, Corot settles down to work. His painting, however, goes poorly as the light changes too frequently.

Patient as ever, Corot returns nine mornings in a row, planting himself in front of his easel at the side of the road.

On the ninth day the sun is gloomy.

The painter hesitates.

He adds some reflections to the water, a mere dab of yellow, when his young companion stops his arm: Papa Corot, do not touch anything!

Somewhat disconcerted, Corot stops.

Then, he agrees: You are right, little one, let us go.

He has caught it, the impression of morning. On the canvas, the sky has merged with the land.

False

Corot can be an unconventional man. When a mediocre or cunning painter asks his advice, he places the offered canvas on his easel and, while humming a merry tune, he bathes the dull and lifeless trees in light.

In five minutes it is done.

How about a signature? asks Corot. All he needs is a timid "yes," and he puts the five letters of his name at the bottom of the canvas.

He also lends his works to young students who copy them for practice.

Do some of them sign with his name? Who knows. Camille does not pay much attention.
And when his misty landscapes become so fashionable that merchants pester him with commissions, he doesn't hesitate to appeal to his assistants.
A few last touches from the Master's paintbrush and the transformation is complete.
This time it is the merchant who isn't attentive enough.
True, false, half-false, a quarter false...
It is a real puzzle, with everything jumbled together.
How mysterious Corot is.

Yport

1870. There is war.

Paris is under siege and during the long months, Corot remains in his studio.

Within his four walls, he "creates Corot's" so as to fulfill commissions.

"I have produced much this winter," he writes, almost with regret. He misses his past adventures. Corot needs the smell of the fields, the immensity of the sea and of the sky.

As early as the following spring, he returns to the road, wishing to see and paint everything again. He reaches the shores of Manche and arrives in July at the village of Yport, which is near Etretat.

With the cliffs before him, their imposing white facades above the sea, everything appears simple to him. By doing a few studies, Corot recovers the enthusiasm of his beginnings.

Through his hand to the tip of his paintbrush, he knows air and light. He has come to know them by heart.

A friend with whom Corot stays, near Yport.

a**Z**ur

Azure

Corot is very sick.

His last works, however, show no sign of that. A warm sun tints the stones of the cathedral the color of old ivory.

A bouquet of flowers blooms on the corner of a table.

An old monk plays the cello.

To Alfred, he confides: "I notice things which I have never seen. It seems to me

that I have never known how to
create a sky.
What is before me is rosier, deeper,
more transparent."
On February 22, 1875, he gently
pushes away the meal which his old
maid, Adèle, serves him.
It will be of no use today.
Father Corot will lunch above, in the
azure heaven of painters.

List of Illustrations

1842, Department of Graphic Arts, Musée du Louvre, Paris. Photo RMN. *Saint-André du Morvan, (Nièvre),* painting, 1842, Musée du Louvre, Paris. Photo from RMN/Lewandowski.

Pages 28-29: *La Rochelle, Entry to the Docks,* painting, 1851, Musée du Louvre, Paris. Photo from RMN/Jean. *The Port of La Rochelle,* 1851, Yale University Art Gallery, New Haven.

Pages 30-31: *A Farm in Nièvre,* painting, 1831, Museum of Fine Arts, Boston.

Pages 32-33: Pencil sketches of dancers, done at the theater, c. 1855–60, from *L'Oeuvre de Corot par Alfred Robaut, Paris,* Floury, 1905. Photo by Roger Viollet. *The Dance of Nymphs,* painting 1850–51, Musée d'Orsay, Paris. Photo from RMN/Lewandowski.

Pages 34-35: *The Roman Odalisque,* or *Marietta,* painting, 1843, Musée du Petit Palais, Paris.

Pages 36-37: *Corot in His Studio* by Bénédict Masson, painting, 1874, private collection. Photo by Roger-Viollet. *Octave Chamouillet,* black-lead sketch, private collection. *The Bride (The Maid-Servant of the Painter Cibot),* painting, c. 1845, Musée du Louvre, Paris. Photo from RMN/Scormans.

Pages 38-39: *The Giving of Prizes on the Closing Day of the Universal Exhibition of 1855,* engraving, Viollet photo collection. The Dale, painting, c. 1850, Musée du Louvre, Paris. Photo from RMN/Arnaudet. *The Cart, Souvenir of Marcoussis,* painting (detail), c. 1855, Musée d'Orsay, Paris. Photo from RMN.

Pages 40-41: *The Belfry of Douai,* painting (detail), 1871, Musée du Louvre, Paris. Photo from RMN/Jean. *The Bridge of Nantes,* painting, c. 1868–70, Musée du Louvre, Paris. Photo from RMN/Jean. *Rider on an Empty Path,* black-lead and black-ink sketch, c. 1870, Musée du Louvre, Paris. Photo from RMN/Berrizi.

Pages 42-43: *Girl at Her Toilet,* painting, 1860-65, Musée du Louvre, Paris. Photo from RMN/Ojéda. *Woman with a Pearl (Portrait of Berthe Goldschmidt in the Pose of Mona Lisa),*

painting, 1868-70, Louvre, Paris. Photo from N/Lewandowski.

Pages 44-45: *Souvenir of Mortefontaine,* painting, 1864, Musée du Louvre, Paris. Photo from RMN/Arnaudet. *Windswept Landscape,* painting (detail), 1865-70, Musées des Beaux-Arts, Reims. Photo by Giraudon. Photograph of Camille Corot by Nadir, about 1870, Bibliothèque Nationale de France, Paris.

Pages 46-47: *Corot and Dutilleux Painting* by Alfred Robaut, drawing, c. 1860, in *L'Oeuvre de Corot par Alfred Robaut,* Paris, Floury, 1905. *Self-Portrait,* engraving (glass plate), 1858, Department of Graphic Arts, Musée du Louvre. Photo from RMN.

Pages 48-49: *Camille Corot Sketching at Ville-d'Avray* by Honré Daumier, watercolor, c. 1860-65, H.-O. Havemeyer Collection, Metropolitan Museum, NY. *The Cabassud Houses at Ville-d'Avray,* painting, c. 1835-40, Musée du Louvre, Paris. Photo from RMN/Lewandowski.

Pages 50-51: *Camille Corot in Saint-Nicolas-les-Arras,* photograph by Charles Desavary, 1873. Photograph of Marissel by Hérbert, 1866. Photo by Roger-Viollet. *The Church of Marissel, Near Beauvais,* painting, 1866, Musée du Louvre, Paris. Photo from RMN/Lewandowski.

Pages 52-53: Signatures of Camille Corot. *Souvenir of Castelgandolfo,* painting (detail), c. 1865, Musée du Louvre, Paris. Photo from RMN/Jean.

Pages 54-55: *Beach and Cliffs at Yport,* painting (detail), 1872, Rijksmuseum Hendrick Willem Mesday, The Hague. *Madame Stumpf and Her Daughter,* painting, 1872, National Gallery of Art, Washington.

Pages 56-57: *The Bridge of Narni,* painting (detail of sky), 1826, Musée du Louvre, Paris. Photo from RMN/Lewandowski. *Flowers in a Glass Beside a Tobacco Jar,* 1874, private collection. *Monk Playing the Cello,* painting, 1874, Kunsthalle, Hamburg.